RAILWAY HERITAGE

DAWN OF THE DIESELS
1956-66
Part 1

RAILWAY HERITAGE

DAWN OF THE DIESELS
1956-66
Part 1

First-generation diesel locomotives and units captured by the camera of

John Spencer Gilks

Edited by Mike Esau

Silver Link Publishing Ltd

First published in February 1998

British Library Cataloguing in Publication Data

A catalogue record for this book is available from the British Library.

ISBN 1 85794 096 2

Silver Link Publishing Ltd
The Trundle
Ringstead Road
Great Addington
Kettering
Northants
NN14 4BW

The number appended to each caption is the negative number. Requests for prints may be made via the Publishers.

Printed and bound in Great Britain

Half title Fulwell & Westbury, Buckinghamshire; Derby 'Lightweight' single car No 79901, 3.45 pm Banbury (Merton Street)-Buckingham, 18 August 1956.
It's high summer, the dawn of the diesels, and all the passengers look happy. Only five days into a totally innovative service, and in a rural area too! They cannot believe their good luck! BR have decided to attempt to retain branch-line traffic in the countryside and have used Buckingham to Banbury as a trial run. Advertising leaflets and more pictures occur on pages 14-18. There were to be eight years before the Government adopted Beeching's recommendation to close the line. 876

Page 2 Lincoln (Central), Lincolnshire; Class 108, 3.32 pm Lincoln (Central)-Doncaster, 18 March 1962.
This is Central station before traffic was diverted there with the closure of St Mark's, a station that has changed little, even to the extent of still having semaphore signals and through lines avoiding the platforms. We've come from Birmingham via Derby, walked over from St Mark's and will go ahead to Doncaster, where we will join the London train. It's a Sunday and we are diverted via the now abandoned north curve at Barkston to travel through Spalding. At Peterborough we hear an announcement - 'Change at Honington for Fort William' - for passengers wishing to join the sleeper. 2586

Title page Towersey, Oxfordshire; Class 118, 12.21 pm Thame-Paddington, 23 April 1962.
Someone has laid the hedge at Towersey, where the train hasn't bothered to call this Easter Sunday. I'm in the car en route to photograph the auto-train that used to push and pull its way from Princes Risborough to Banbury, calling at all stations and halts. *2615*

Opposite page Norton Halt, Hereford & Worcester; Class 116, 6.25 pm Worcester (Shrub Hill)-Evesham, 4 April 1964.
Norton is the junction of the Oxford line with the loop that enables Midland trains to call at Worcester (Shrub Hill). Whilst the route to London is now single track, the box and the semaphore signals remain. *3121*

Below Black Rock Halt, Gwynedd; 27 May 1970.
Alan Lillywhite takes a picture of John Gilks taking his photographs that appear on page 36. C3569

Below right JSG 1993.
At work on his first book. *Gavin Mist*

CONTENTS

Evershot Tunnel, Dorset, near north portal; Class 120, 1.5 pm Westbury-Weymouth, 1 September 1964.
Evershot Tunnel, Dorset, south portal; Class 119, 1.5 pm Bristol (Temple Meads)-Weymouth, 1 September 1964.
I find this tunnel fascinating. At the north end it is preceded by a deep cutting, but when the train emerges there is barely enough hillside to contain the portal. The latter adjoins the main road from Dorchester to Yeovil, newly widened at this location. *3311/3312*

INTRODUCTION

It was on Easter Monday 1958 that I first travelled on diesel trains. In the morning I joined an ex-Great Western railcar at Cheltenham (Malvern Road) and went to Honeybourne, standing all the way to Broadway as there was limited seating accommodation and crowds of people were going out for a day in the Cotswolds to such places as Gretton Halt, Hayles Abbey Halt and Laverton Halt.

At 7.15 pm that evening, in Cambridge, on boarding the Norwich-Liverpool Street express, I was to find at its head what we now term a Class 31 locomotive. It so happened that the Prince of Wales, then nine years of age, had used the down working of this train to reach Ely (and Sandringham?) and was very fond of the rectangular puff-pastry biscuits containing nine slots that oozed strawberry jam. Or so the restaurant car steward informed us over dinner. He therefore had six tins of this confectionery on board and offered us some of the delicious biscuits with our sweet!

Those who have read my first book - *Journeys round Britain* in Silver Link's 'Classic Steam' series - will recognise my trip (see the schedule and map on page 10) as part of the nationwide itinerary I followed with my friends Harry Grenside and Alan Lillywhite to cover the entire BR network as it existed in the ten years or so after 1954. I used to look out of the carriage window for vantage points for photography, then travel back there by car to augment the pictures we had taken on the train journey. Hence the photographs in this book, of which a number marked 'AL' were taken by Alan.

Evidently, as diesel traction took over from steam, many photographers put their cameras away, believing that there was nothing more to record. As my pictures emphasise the train in the scene, I continued as before, and thus have an archive of early diesels, many on routes that later disappeared with the Beeching closures, while stations retained their Steam Age features before rationalisation.

Dawn of the Diesels draws on this collection at the invitation of Will Adams and with the editorial and printing skills of Mike Esau, to both of whom I am indebted and would like to record my sincere thanks.

Two journeys with diesel traction that particularly stay in my mind took place on 18 September 1959 and 18 July 1969 respectively.

The first involved a ride in the cab of the prototype 'Deltic' from King's Cross to Doncaster when heading 'The White Rose' express. This had been arranged by the BBC when I was connected with their Radio 3 magazine programme *On Railways*, and I had a portable - so-called - tape-recorder with me. This could barely handle the intense noise of the locomotive as I climbed into the cab; my ears also had problems coping with the din, and I pondered as to how the staff could live with this racket without illness. Once under way I became accustomed to the atmosphere and enjoyed a briefing by kindly Inspector Dolby whose son I had met during National Service.

Two events stand out. As we approached the peat bog north of Holme speed dropped off and the driver invited me to look at the speedometer. It read 60 mph as compared with the 90 mph from London. We seemed to have stopped - rather like when driving a car into a 30 mph area. How speeds have been raised on the East Coast Main Line since 1959! The other event was the sight of an 'A4' 'Pacific' pulling an up train away from a stop at Retford climbing round the curve towards Gamston. My return journey included a ride on an 'A4' from Grantham to Peterborough - on a full stomach, as there had actually been time for lunch from Doncaster! The recordings on the footplate were not good as the loco - No 60029 *Woodcock* - was due for shops and rocked alarmingly!

The second journey arose from proposals to reorganise local government that had been published in July 1969, and my professional career took me to a speaking engagement in Kidderminster on the 18th. The leader of the Council was Station Manager at Birmingham (New Street) and met me there when changing trains. The DMU was full of squealing school-kids, so he arranged for me to sit in the front with the driver. This was great as I

Above In the Introduction to my first book (*Journeys round Britain* in Silver Link's 'Classic Steam' series, published in 1994) I mentioned the bridge in King Charles's Road, Surbiton, from which I first looked at the trains from my pushchair. Mike has now located this picture by Geoff Rixon of an up freight taken from the bridge.

Left John and Alan on location. Despite appearances, the cable release fires only the shutter!

could enjoy the sight of the complicated junctions at this interchange station and the route through Stourbridge. Next day I attended one of the first meetings of the Board of the embryo Severn Valley Railway.

A great advantage of the new diesel multiple units - on which I made my first journey, from Norwich City to Melton Constable, on 4 August 1958 - was the front view provided for the passenger. Not only did this emulate the front seat upstairs on a bus, but also opened eyes to the features of the system and the marvels of Victorian engineering. More's the pity that some parents failed to discipline children when they banged on the window behind the driver, leading him to pull down the blind to assist his concentration - and giving an opportunity to those less charitable drivers to be awkward to passengers - and the loss of this amenity in the later design of train.

As I mentioned in my first book, but was unable to elaborate on because of its emphasis on steam, I had the privilege of hiring the General Manager's Saloon from York for private charters with members of the 'Talking of Trains' evening class (of Surbiton in Surrey) and later for the Friends of the National Railway Museum. This was a diesel multiple unit fitted out with boardroom, bar, settees and armchairs. I have devoted a chapter to this sub-

ject (page 88). Enhanced facilities provided for us later in Scotland included a dining and kitchen car, and required diesel haulage.

The first GM's Saloon we hired had been built by D. Wickham & Company Ltd of Ware in Hertfordshire. My first journey by rail other than behind steam had been provided by the same company in the form of a petrol-engined vehicle on which the Army allowed Hugh Davies and myself to travel from Shrewsbury (Abbey Foregate) station to Llanymynech along the former Shropshire & Montgomeryshire Railway on 17 August 1953. We took nearly 6 hours to travel the 18 miles or so (including a digression to near Criggion on a single line already occupied by another train).

Although I didn't travel by diesel, as far as I can recall, until 1958, I had photographed my first, ex-Great Western railcar No 7, at Chipping Norton on 30 April 1955 (see the accompanying photograph), and my second, BR single unit No 79900, at Padbury on 18 August 1956 (see page 16).

The first railway enthusiast diesel tour, using an ex-

My first diesel photograph: ex-Great Western Railcar No W7W forming a Kingham train at Chipping Norton, Oxon, 30 April 1955. 506

Circular Tour: 7 April 1958

Guildford	dep	7.50 am	Leamington Spa (General)	arr	2.23
Reading (Southern)	arr	8.50	Leamington Spa (Milverton)	dep	2.43
Reading (General)	dep	9.02			
Oxford	arr	9.42	*Via Daventry and Blisworth (reverse)*		
	dep	10.02	Northampton (Castle)	arr	4.01
Kingham	arr	10.27		dep	4.24
	dep	10.37	Wellingborough (Midland Rd)	arr	4.48
Cheltenham (Malvern Road)	arr	11.30		dep	4.58
	dep	11.35	Kettering	arr	5.09
Honeybourne	arr	12.25 pm		dep	5.25
	dep	12.34	Cambridge	arr	7.03
Evesham	arr	12.45		dep	7.15
Reverse			London (Liverpool Street)	arr	8.46
	dep	1.14	London (Waterloo)	dep	9.50
Via Stratford-upon-Avon and Hatton			Guildford	arr	10.26 pm

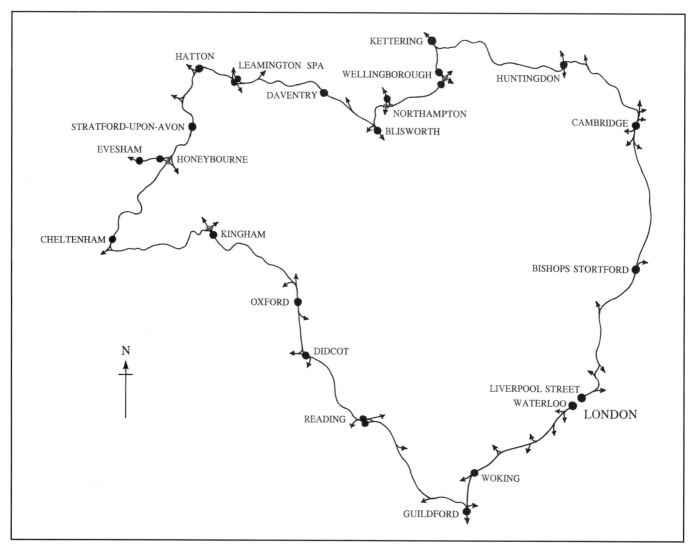

A map of the 7 April 1958 tour, which would become impossible just over a year later
when the Kettering-Huntingdon line was closed to passengers.

Right 'The Devon Rambler' railtour, 11 April 1959.

GWR railcar, was organised by the Birmingham Locomotive Club to Welshpool on 2 July 1949. The first to employ a BR DMU was 'The Devon Rambler', on which I travelled from Plymouth to Yealmpton and Turnchapel, chartered by the Railway Enthusiasts' Club on 11 April 1959. As the accompanying handbill shows, this was not universally popular with the membership.

Some nuts and bolts to finish this Introduction. The caption to each picture begins with its location (using station names from 1955 and local government areas as in April 1974), then details of the locomotive and its train, and the date on which it was taken, when known; finally there is more detail of the scene and the circumstances in which it was recorded. I am grateful to John Edgington for letting me take advantage of his vast knowledge of detail, so willingly given, and to Don Smith for his ingenuity with my ancient computer. Also Phil Atkins and his team at the NRM for providing me with outline timetables.

To return to the opening sentence. You may wonder how I went by train from Honeybourne to Cambridge on 7 April 1958, having first driven my Morris Minor from Kingston (then my home town) to Guildford to pick up Alan and join Harry, and this is set out in the table opposite (only stations where changes occurred are shown). The itinerary was typical of the way we covered most of the BR network - 'three men in a train' - with Circular Tour Tickets to reduce the cost. I hope you will enjoy the outcome as narrated and illustrated in this book.

John Gilks
Nawton, 1997

RAILWAY ENTHUSIASTS' CLUB
FARNBOROUGH   -   HANTS

* * * * * * * * * * * * * * * * * * * *

ITINERARY
OF
"THE DEVON RAMBLER"

EXETER ST. DAVIDS - LYDFORD - LAIRA YARD - FRIARY
YEALMPTON - TURNCHAPEL TUNNEL - ST. BUDEAUX - MILLBAY
DAWLISH - EXETER

Saturday, 11th April, 1959

W E L C O M E
                    to all our members and their guests, and
to all our other friends travelling on this train, including our
fellow enthusiasts of the Plymouth Railway Circle.

    We sincerely hope that you all enjoy this trip today - and
that we may have the pleasure of your company on other R.E.C.
trips in the future.

    The use of a cross-country diesel set on this tour has brought
forth a spate of correspondence commenting on our choice of motive
power and stock - some critical (often very so) but many more
complimentary.

    We thank you for your interest, and for giving us your views,
very often with much useful additional information. It is quite
clear that the majority of railway enthusiasts, whilst in varying
degrees mourning the passing of the steam locomotive, are ready
and anxious to recognise the presence of diesel traction by using
it in - at present at least - moderate degree on rail tour trains.

    For those who pine for steam, a glance at the future programme
of the club will prove that "puffers" are not forgotten.

    By the way, IF British Railways have failed to put the first
class at the front leading out of Exeter, please don't ask the
organisers to turn the train round ! We did our best.

    May we remind you that refreshments will be on sale throughout
the tour from the buffet in the centre of the train; and most
standard types of films for your camera will be on sale at the
R.E.C. enquiry desk, also near the centre of the train. Here you
may also book for future trips, and other enquiries will be dealt
with.

                        THE RAIL TOUR COMMITTEE
                            M.G. Langdon
                            R.P.S. Bevin
                            H. Davies

Hull, Anlaby Road Curve; six-car hybrid DMU; 1.15 pm Scarborough-Leicester; 2 September 1989.
Dusk of the first generation DMUs - a photograph taken when they were about to be called 'Heritage units'.
This is also the last running of this particular service.

1.
DAWN OF THE DIESELS

The first days of August 1956, the month when the diesel units began commercial operation in the South of England, were busy ones for me. I was drafting the itinerary for 'The Suffolk Venturer' of the Railway Enthusiasts' Club and my advance advertising led to a booking by a representative of Fisons, the fertiliser people, who saw a way of gaining access to Hadleigh station on a Sunday when staff were absent, to see how their products were being stored. On Bank Holiday Monday (then at the beginning of the month) a circular railtour took me to Dulverton and the route from Newton Abbot to Exeter via Christow.

The next day, 7 August, I was on the first re-instated train from Lewes to East Grinstead and met Miss Bessemer, who had been instrumental in forcing the Southern Region to restore the service following an illegal closure. This was a significant day and was to be an object lesson to BR management as to how to handle the public relations of a closure - which some of them learned in time for Beeching - and which led eventually to today's preserved Bluebell Railway.

On the 18th I went to see the new DMUs in service in Buckinghamshire. As I didn't yet possess a car, my Uncle Fred, a retired bus driver, took me there in his Austin 10 with the far-sighted registration number BMC 48! At Fulwell & Westbury we met my friend Nigel who, sadly, we were to lose in his teens from epilepsy. He is the young man in the first picture in this book, having just alighted from the train; he really loved my uncle's old car.

I have included perhaps a disproportionate number of the pictures taken that day, but make no apology as I cannot stress too much how significant this moment was for branch lines and travel in the countryside. It was a positive step by BR in their modernisation plan to introduce the new diesel units. They experimented to see whether by lowering the costs of operation (reduction in signalling and the number of passing loops required did not come until much later and perforce elsewhere) branch lines could be retained in competition with the growing number of motor cars and bus services that we know with hindsight were at their peak level in 1953. In the event the Buckingham service was swept away as an embarrassing nuisance after only eight years; in 1956 the positive railwaymen held sway, but by 1964 politicians within railway management, and outside, had taken over.

On that August Saturday, as you can see, we visited all the stations between Padbury (page 16) and Farthinghoe (page 17), including the new halts at Water Stratford and Radclive (page 15); the latter adjoined the distinguished house and estate of that name. Little did I realise then that in due course, when I became a Liveryman of the Worshipful Company of Carmen and a Freeman of the City of London, I would shake hands with its owner across the top table!

My first visit to Verney Junction was with Hugh Davies on 12 February 1955, with snow all around, when preparing an article for the REC Journal. The Station Master met us and authorised me to climb the ladders of the lofty junction signal posts so as to gain better vantage points for photography. This was my first experience of this procedure and I can still recall how slippery it was, how cold and icy up there and how my fingers froze. The pictures - of steam trains - appeared in the June 1955 Journal. We were told how servicemen used to spend hours here between trains because of inefficient Orderly Room staff wrongly routing their railway passes and how, in vain, the Station Master advised the Army of the error of its ways, while continuing to stoke up the waiting room fire to keep the soldiers warm.

In its heyday trains with Pullman cars from Liverpool Street (Metropolitan) would terminate at Verney Junction in the evening, having set down most of their business clientele at Aylesbury. The very first railtour with members of my 'Talking of Trains' evening class at Surbiton - five of us - from Staines West to Euston via Uxbridge (Vine Street), Marlow and Monks Risborough involved a taxi from Calvert to Verney Junction in the middle of the afternoon of 14 April 1964. This was to lead to more than a score of charter trains.

The pictures at Godstone and Woldingham (page 21) bring back memories. In the first case I am killing time while on the way to dinner at his home in Sevenoaks with the BBC producer of the *On Railways* programme. People find it hard to believe that I am very shy, but it is so, and in those days I was not so accustomed to having dinner out. Accordingly I am rather dreading the evening, which, of course, worked out fine.

Below Stewkley, Buckinghamshire; Derby 'Lightweight' single cars Nos 79900 and 79901, 12.30 pm Bletchley-Banbury, 19 September 1957.
It's Thursday and Alan and I have taken a day's leave from work to see how the new DMUs are getting on. The two single cars are coupled together to get them from Bletchley to the branch. They still look reasonably pristine! AL950

I must have had a long lunch-hour from my job at County Hall, Kingston, to visit Woldingham, and I'm looking for a vantage point to photograph the Lingfield Race Special that followed this stopping train. My car must have taken flight as I decided to head up the line to Upper Warlingham and was there in time to see the special (12.52 pm ex-Victoria). This conveyed Pullman cars at the rear for lunch and, it was said, to enable the bookmakers to make a quick getaway at the London barrier after the races.

Below right Radclive, Buckinghamshire; Derby 'Lightweight' single car; 2.55 pm Buckingham-Banbury, 18 August 1956.
The London Midland Region not only provided new trains but two new halts as well. Here is Radclive, which adjoined the village of that name but had been ignored by trains for more than 100 years! Illumination was still provided by oil lamps despite electricity overhead to the cottage. 876

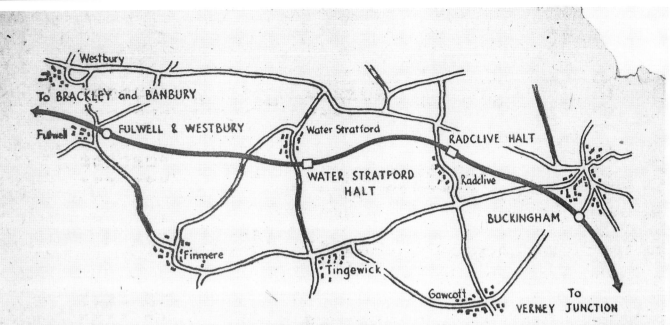

LOCATION OF NEW HALTS AT RADCLIVE AND WATER STRATFORD

Now!

AD160

DIESEL TRAINS

BETWEEN

BUCKINGHAM

AND

BANBURY

STARTING 13th AUGUST 1956

NEW TRAINS — MORE TRAINS
NEW HALTS AT

RADCLIVE and WATER STRATFORD

FOR FULL DETAILS OF IMPROVED SERVICES ALSO ALTERED TRAIN
SERVICES BETWEEN BLETCHLEY AND BUCKINGHAM—SEE INSIDE

BRITISH RAILWAYS

Left The handbill advertising the new diesel train service.

Below Padbury, Buckinghamshire; Derby 'Lightweight' single car, 12.33 pm Winslow-Banbury, 18 August 1956.
As stated in the Introduction, this is my first picture of a British Railways diesel. I wonder whether the lady porter also tends the well-kept garden. 872

Right Farthinghoe, Northamptonshire; Derby 'Lightweight' single car, 5.25 pm Banbury-Buckingham, 18 August 1956.
This station closed to passengers on 3 November 1952 and, strangely enough, was not re-opened when the DMUs arrived, although it is quite close to the village. Had our previous Deputy Prime Minister lived close by at that time, the situation might have been different. 878

Below right Buckingham, Buckinghamshire; Derby 'Lightweight' single car No 79901, 1.30 pm Banbury-Buckingham, 18 August 1956.
Buckingham station became an interchange point between steam and diesel during the experimental period. This train has come from Banbury and terminated. 873

AD164

ALTERED and IMPROVED
TRAIN SERVICES

BETWEEN

BLETCHLEY

AND

BUCKINGHAM

STARTING 13th AUGUST 1956

DIESEL TRAIN SERVICES BETWEEN BUCKINGHAM
AND BANBURY BEGIN ON THE SAME DAY

FOR DETAILS OF THE REVISED SERVICES PLEASE SEE OTHER SIDE

BRITISH RAILWAYS

Left The handbill advertising the 'altered and improved' diesel service between Bletchley and Buckingham.

Below Verney Junction, Buckinghamshire; Derby 'Lightweight' single car, 1.37 pm Buckingham-Bletchley, 16 March 1963.
My favourite station, as readers of my first book will be aware, was Verney Junction, named after the local landowner because no community existed at that location. The Oxford-Bletchley line was to be part of a freight route avoiding London and a flyover crossing the West Coast Main Line was provided. A freight train is awaiting a path after the DMU, which has just left the Buckingham line on the right; note that the unit has a yellow patch on the end. Today only a rusty single line passes through the undergrowth from Bletchley to Claydon. *AL1070*

Claydon, Buckinghamshire; Class 114, 1.48 pm Bletchley-Oxford, 13 August 1960.

This piece of line, though singled, still handles a refuse train from Bristol, which reverses beyond this bridge and climbs the wartime Calvert spur to reach what remains of the Great Central, which used to pass above on its way north. The rubbish is tipped into disused clay pits. *2148*

Gamlingay, Cambridgeshire; Class 108, 2.00 pm Bletchley-Cambridge, 21 March 1962.
The porter advised me that substantial quantities of straw mats were sent by rail from here, but the traffic was discouraged when closure was a possibility.
Also the most profitable train on the line - the 6.00 pm from Ipswich to Cardiff, carrying Birds Eye frozen products - was diverted via Temple Mills.
The station closed on 1 January 1968. 2590

Right Godstone, Surrey; Class 207, 6.30 pm Redhill-Tonbridge, 3 September 1963.
This station is 3 miles from the town it serves and a separate community has grown around it. Until recently the trains still adopted the pattern laid down by the South Eastern Railway and connected Reading with Tonbridge. Since electrification the basic service links Maidstone West with Three Bridges and in addition there is an hourly fast train between Tunbridge Wells and Victoria. 2985

Below Woldingham, Surrey; Class 207, 12.31 pm London (Victoria)-Tunbridge Wells via East Grinstead, 24 August 1962.
This station has the distinction of a public path over the footbridge and a door in the wall of the up platform where it enters Marden Park. There is a tall LB&SCR lower-quadrant signal for London trains. The train is strengthened to carry office workers home from London at Saturday lunchtime. 2750

Above Charing, Kent; Class 201, 6.19 pm, Maidstone East-Ashford, 11 March 1961.
During preparations for electrification a 'Hastings' diesel was pressed into service between Maidstone East and Ashford. Note the bicycles in the rack and the pile of mailbags on the right. *2386*

Opposite page Purton (near the Severn Bridge), Gloucestershire; Class 120, 8.25 am Birmingham (Snow Hill)-Carmarthen, 6 May 1958.
This train is running by way of Stratford-on-Avon and Gloucester, as shown in the advertisement for 1960/61. *AL1056*

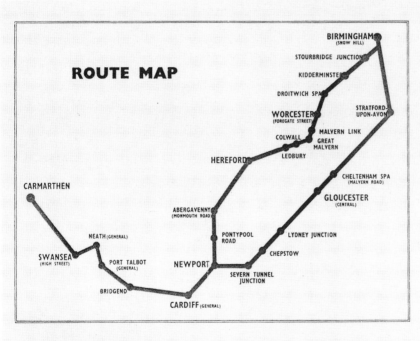

ROUTE MAP

Through DIESEL
& Steam Train Services

BIRMINGHAM—
SOUTH WALES

12th September, 1960
to 11th June, 1961
or until further notice

WESTERN REGION

2.
NORTH DEVON AND CORNWALL

This is the first of four chapters illustrating diesel trains in specific parts of the UK.

In my opinion a real tragedy, with long-term effects far wider than the railway scene, took place on 1 January 1963. On that day the British Transport Commission was abolished, and when designating areas for the new Regional Railway Boards that were set up, the Southern Region network west of Wilton (by Salisbury) was transferred to the Western Region. I have yet to discover who conceived this idea. Presumably, if logic was involved, the Southern was regarded as a London Commuter system and its continued extension into the West Country was an historic anachronism. But the progenitor did not reckon with bigoted senior men at Paddington who saw their last opportunity to destroy the 19th-century competitor. It was ironical that Stanley Raymond had arrived at Paddington as the WR's General Manager in January 1962 with an instruction to flush out this old guard, but presumably he indulged in empire-building like the next man. Perhaps it was his idea!

In any case it took no time to ruin the express service from Waterloo to Exeter. The 11 am down, which had been the proud 'Atlantic Coast Express' with through portions to various branch lines in North Cornwall for the convenience of passengers, was cut back to Salisbury for no obvious reason. The dining cars were removed and people were encouraged to travel from Paddington and contribute to Western Region coffers. While public opinion, especially in north Dorset, would not let them totally disregard the Southern route to Exeter (though it was reduced to single track for the most part) there was presumably less political clout west of that city, and the network there has all but disappeared. Only the line to Barnstaple continues to survive, although in the summer of 1997 an experimental passenger service was introduced to Okehampton on the former route to Plymouth and Padstow. This line was retained as far as Meldon Quarry for stone traffic.

Sadly I had rarely driven in the area in question. My Morris Minor seemed to slow down markedly west of Exeter and I postponed my journeys until I had a more powerful car. This is fortunate for this book as my pictures show the diesel units that the Western Region operated there in the last days. It is a kind of epitaph for the main line over Dartmoor and the Bude and Padstow branches.

You may well ask why they are preceded by a picture of a DMU on its way to Kingswear. The answer is the condition of the permanent way, the formation and the unit itself. Impeccable! Preservation of the natural environment has not yet been used as an excuse for lack of maintenance.

Churston, Devon; Class 117 (x3), 9.30 am Newton Abbot-Kingswear, 10 July 1960.
This picture is included to demonstrate how clean and tidy the permanent way was maintained prior to financial economies masquerading as respect for the natural environment. The train, too, is spotless and is made up of three three-car sets. It is Sunday morning on a line that transferred on 1 November 1972 to a preservation group. The distance from Paddington via Bristol is indicated in the foreground. *2110*

Left Brentor, Devon; Class 117, 3.39 pm Exeter (Central)-Plymouth, 1 July 1966.
Today this station has been transformed into a really charming country house with its garden along the permanent way. At the time of this photograph it was still oil-lit. Above the waiting shelter on the right the course of the former Great Western branch from Plymouth to Launceston can be seen; this ran parallel with the Southern from north of Tavistock to Lydford, where a wartime connection was inserted. *3610*

Below left Lydford, Devon; Class 117, 11.30 am Plymouth-Exeter (Central), 2 July 1966.
The above-mentioned connection is behind the camera to the south, and has been used by 'The Devon Rambler' of the Railway Enthusiasts' Club (see page 11). The Great Western engine shed survives in the distance and the track towards Launceston is intact. *3615*

Above right Bridestowe, Devon; Class 117, 5.22 pm Exeter (Central)-Plymouth, 2 July 1966.
We are going along the line northwards and Dartmoor is clearly visible on the horizon. The track in the goods yard has been lifted but the loading gauge remains. Goods traffic ended here in 1961, and the passenger service was discontinued in 1968. *3616*

Below Meldon Junction, Devon; Class 116 running as two-car set, Okehampton-Bude, 1 July 1966.
On the right is the main line from Exeter (Cowley Bridge Junction) south towards Plymouth, and the train has diverged for Ashbury and Halwill Junction, where it will take the line to Bude (as opposed to Padstow or Torrington). Meldon Quarry is just below the horizon on the left. *3611*

Ashbury, Devon; Class 116 running as two-car set, Okehampton-Bude, 1 July 1966.
Here tickets were obtained from the signal box, and there is a Victorian letter box in the station wall on the extreme left. The picture was taken during a tour by car of the area over a four-day period when the daylight was at its longest. *3607*

Dunsland Cross, Devon; Class 122, Okehampton-Bude, 1 July 1966.
The passing loop has no signals and is disused. Indeed, the station looks totally run down, and was closed on 3 October 1966. The station building has now been converted to an attractive guest house. *3606*

Holsworthy, Devon; Class 116 running as two-car set, Okehampton-Bude, 30 June 1966.
As we move station to station westwards along the Bude branch, we reach Holsworthy, where the passing loop survives and the signalman is exchanging the single-line token with the driver. *3603*

Whitstone & Bridgerule, Devon; Class 116 running as two-car set, Bude-Okehampton, 30 June 1966.
The name of this station always brings to mind a piece of scientific equipment used in the laboratory! Looking down from a bridge of great height sprung across the cutting, it's surprising to see that the loop is still in use, bearing in mind the relatively short distance between Halwill and Holsworthy. *3604*

Above left Egloskerry, Cornwall; Class 122, Padstow-Halwill Junction, 30 June 1966.
We are now on the North Cornwall line west of Launceston. The station buildings are more substantial here to guard against the prevailing wild climate - note the slate facing on one wall. *3602*

Left Tresmeer, Cornwall; Class 122, Halwill Junction-Padstow, 30 June 1966.
Never have I been more conscious of a quieter place to await the arrival of an evening train. There was total silence before the diesel unit stole under the bridge; no one got on or off, and it then disappeared away to the south. Note that there are no station lamps, barrows or seats. In fact, the station was closed in all but name; there had been no staff here for the previous 18 months. It is hard to believe that the 'Atlantic Coast Express' called here for London each weekday prior to the Western Region take-over. *3605*

Above Otterham, Cornwall; Class 122, Padstow-Halwill Junction, 1 July 1966.
At one time the station had a passing loop, which appears to have just been lifted. This location can be very bleak. *3608*

3.
WALES

Permission had been granted to close the Carmarthen-Aberystwyth line from 22 February 1965, despite the sequel that no train could then go from South Wales to North Wales without a sortie into England. More than 34 miles were retained, however, at the southern end for milk traffic from Pont Llanio (and from Felin Fach on the Aberayron branch and MoD traffic on the Newcastle Emlyn branch).

Although rather more recent than most of the photographs included in this book, the milk trains were still running in 1970, so on the morning of Saturday 23 May we enquired of station staff at Carmarthen whether there would be one that weekend. They advised us to come back at about 3 o'clock, by which time they should have had a telephone message from the Milk Marketing Board at Thames Ditton (near my Kingston home). In the event there were four tankers to pick up on Sunday. We were staying in Newcastle Emlyn and after lunch drove across to Bryn Teify to see the light engine go north. Having done so we settled ourselves in the meadow knowing that it must return, hence the picture. Running such a train on a Sunday must have been a costly exercise. A month earlier I had run a DMU over these lines in connection with the Blue Pullman from Surbiton.

Another Welsh line retained long after formal closure is that through the Vale of Glamorgan. Passenger services over it to Bridgend ended in 1961, and to Llantwit Major in 1964; they were then cut back to Barry, but engineering work on the main line often sees trains diverted this way still from Cardiff at weekends.

The Central Wales line has been threatened with closure many times, but today it is in better shape than for years thanks to the interest in it of the Prince of Wales. Indeed, recently heavy steel trains were diverted this way during bridge reconstruction on the main line near Bridgend, so the structures must be sound. I have included three pictures in this book.

Happily the loops have been restored at Llandrindod Wells station and at Knighton; the latter was much

delayed for although the town is in Wales the station is in England, so the Welsh Office grant could not be used. An approach to the English local authorities for help met with a rebuff - they had no interest in subsidising a Welsh community! The engineer was asked to consider resiting the station across the river, but the prevailing gradient meant that this was impossible without vast cost. Eventually common sense must have prevailed as the loop is in place again, ending the years when one single-track section stretched for over 30 miles from Craven Arms to Llandrindod Wells. I have allowed myself one picture of the Central Wales in England to recall the time when east of Knighton the formation was double track.

It's Wednesday at Black Rock Sands so the loss-making weekly goods is returning from Pwllheli; normally it turned back at the explosives depot at Penrhyndeudraeth. Up in the mountains to the east trains are making their way from Llandudno to Blaenau Ffestiniog; two views show the magnificent scenery between Roman Bridge and the north portal of the tunnel that leads to the town. Could there ever be a greater contrast in the natural environment than between the two ends of this tunnel?

Above right Llanpumpsaint, Dyfed; Class 35, Pont Llanio-Carmarthen milk, 24 May 1970.
The circumstances in which this picture was taken are described in the text. *3685*

Right Llantwit Major, South Glamorgan; Class 119, 1.35 pm Barry-Llantwit Major, 21 May 1961.
There has been much talk about restoring a normal passenger service here from Cardiff, particularly as the airport adjoins the line, and there would seem good reason to divert the Barry Island service here, except on Bank Holiday weekends when the car parks are full (radio news flash, August Bank Holiday 1996). Diverted expresses pass this way regularly when engineering works so dictate. *2426*

Above **Pontrhydyfen, West Glamorgan; Class 116, 11.36 am Treherbert-Neath, 1 June 1962.**
I'm driving indirectly from Pontypool to Dursley and wait for this train as the scenery is good. This picture has been published before, when a reader advised me of my incorrect caption. I hope that I have got it right now! The train has came through Blaenrhondda Tunnel from Treherbert and is on the Rhondda & Swansea Bay Railway to Aberavon. In the background is the Port Talbot Railway. *2685*

Left Llandrindod Wells, Powys; Class 37, 3.00 pm Shrewsbury-Swansea.
Above right Llangunllo, Powys; Class 120, 12.25 pm Shrewsbury-Swansea.
Right Bucknell, Shropshire; Class 120, 5.50 am Swansea-Shrewsbury, all 17 July 1965.
These three pictures were all taken on the Central Wales, with one in England; I talk about them on page 32. *3483/3482/3480*

Black Rock Halt, Gwynedd; Class 101, Pwllheli-Machynlleth; Class 24, Pwllheli-Penrhyndeudraeth, both 27 May 1970.
These pictures were taken from the same spot as that taken by Alan on page 4. Snowdonia is to the north and Criccieth Castle to the west.
Despite many attempts to close the line it survives, primarily for the conveyance of school children
(like the Esk Valley line to Whitby). 3688/3689

Right Llangybi, Gwynedd; Derby 'Lightweight', 4.04 pm Bangor-Pwllheli, 22 May 1962.
It looks as though the platforms have been reconstructed in concrete, so perhaps the original wooden ones became unsafe. There is a small London & North Western signal box and a lower-quadrant signal for the train. *2650*

Below Mostyn, Clwyd; Class 101, 4.30 pm Chester-Bangor, 3 June 1965.
The station building on the right was provided by the Chester & Holyhead Railway at its opening in 1848. A steel works dominates the background. *3457*

Above Roman Bridge, Gwynedd; Class 101, Llandudno-Blaenau Ffestiniog, 24 September 1966.
Below Ffestiniog Tunnel, near north end, Gwynedd; Class 101, Llandudno-Blaenau Ffestiniog, 28 May 1970.
In the first picture a friend of mine is standing by the house on the right and I can hear his speech perfectly because of the peace of the place and the response of the mountain echo. The train approaching the tunnel in the second view is an experimental Sunday service operated under contract to Gwynedd County Council. *3631/3690*

4.
EASTERN ENGLAND

After the original Buckingham experiment, many of the new DMUs seemed to be concentrated in the East of England to replace steam locos and rolling-stock that were very much life-expired. Hence many of my early pictures were taken here. For convenience of selection I have enlarged the geographical area in just a few cases to extend as far west as Welham Junction and as far north as Driffield.

Alan took the picture at Colchester on page 42 the day in 1959 that we went to Brightlingsea. You can surmise from the date of several of the views that I explored the East Suffolk line on 13 July 1963, having been to Wickham Market the previous day. I have since seen buses meet the school children there and take them from the train to the town - it was not by chance that the station used to be called 'for Campsea Ash' from its true location - and outlying villages, a happy arrangement. Eastern Region General Manager Gerard Fiennes was to use this route as an experiment in his 'basic railway operation' concept, but that was still in the future at the time of our visit.

It's a route that dispels the popular myth that Suffolk is flat; the formation goes up and down incessantly with many curves to ease gradients, and gravity was of great assistance to old steam locos on heavy holiday trains to Lowestoft and Yarmouth in seeking to maintain their schedule. Brampton station was said to have been spared closure at the whim of the local MP, a one-time member of the Cabinet. Could this be the reason why on a more recent visit I discovered that the station was omitted from the printed timetable on display and that a small piece of paper had been inserted in the frame stating the running times from adjacent stations?

The train passing Acle (page 45) is typical of the many summer Saturday services that used to serve the East Coast from the Midlands and the North, so much longer than the daily DMU and sometimes overlapping the loops on the single lines. This was particularly true of the Midland & Great Northern lines, remembered in the pic-

ture of Whitwell & Reepham (also page 45), with its overloaded system in high summer. Trains had to set back into goods sidings.

I find it hard to understand why the service from Norwich to King's Lynn was withdrawn, in 1968. There is a great deal of business between the two places, with Dereham en route for good measure, not to mention Swaffham, which bustles with activity and brought in rail traffic from Watton and Thetford. I have included three illustrations. The only explanation for closure seems to be, like York direct to Hull, that each Region had to lose, say, 10 per cent of its services to satisfy some Beeching (Margetts) criteria, and that this is how the Eastern contributed its share.

The holiday train at Sandy in Bedfordshire (page 48) is diverted from its usual route because of a problem at Whittlesea (between Peterborough and March) that day. The picture on page 49 allows us to see what Lord's Bridge station, on the Oxford-Cambridge route, looked like before the Mullard Laboratory took over.

There are three pictures between Peterborough and Rugby. Welham Junction marks the spot at which the LNWR/GNR Joint Line took off for Newark and Nottingham; the marshalling yard there must have been very windswept and inhospitable, especially in the early hours of the morning. The scene at Cotham is probably a unique photograph, as few trains passed this way after 11 September 1939 - a wartime closure - except the goods, which survived until recent years. A DMU there is almost a mirage!

Barnetby (page 53) has proved to be almost the last country junction with such a multitude of signals (some controlled from Wrawby Junction box), though the platform buildings have been replaced. The former main line to Manchester has passenger trains on Saturdays only, but the routes to Lincoln and Doncaster are still busy. Indeed, east of the station traffic is such that one of the tracks removed under rationalisation has had to be restored. There's hope for the railways yet!

Woodham Ferrers, Essex; Class 116, 11.01 am Wickford-Southminster, 12 October 1963.

Until 1939 passenger trains linked Maldon East with Woodham Ferrers via Cold Norton; indeed, freight kept going until at least 1953. Since the Second World War this part of Essex has seen considerable housing development and the Southminster branch is now electrified. This is London commuter country, the home of 'Essex man'! 3019

Left Colchester, Essex; Class 31 No D5520, 3.38 pm Liverpool Street-Yarmouth (South Town), 3 May 1959.
This is the day of our visit to railways in the Tendring Hundred, including the closed Brightlingsea branch. Although the burrowing under the main line of the down Clacton track has been completed and electrification from the bay on the left at Colchester, the London trains, like the one arriving here, are still diesel-hauled. There has often been argument about the relative importance of buses and cars in the parking arrangements at this station. *AL1062*

Below Wickham Market, Suffolk; Derby 'Lightweight'/Metro-Cammell 'Lightweight', 10.30 am Yarmouth (South Town)-Ipswich and vice versa, 12 July 1963.
I like this picture taken in the days before the East Suffolk Railway was reduced to a single track under Gerry Fiennes's 'basic railway operation'. Until 1952 (1965 for goods) this was the junction for the Framlingham branch (note the island platform), which diverged westwards a little to the north of the station. *2908*

Halesworth, Suffolk; Derby 'Lightweight', 2.30 pm Yarmouth (South Town)-Ipswich, 13 July 1963.
The next day I visited Halesworth. 'For Southwold' reads the station sign, and indeed until 1929 you could have travelled there by train on the Southwold Railway. At this time the passenger trains ran ahead from Beccles (junction for Bungay, etc, until 1953/1964) to Yarmouth via Haddiscoe; now they turn there on a single line to Oulton Broad and terminate in Lowestoft. Note the tank wagons in the sidings. 2910

Left Brampton, Suffolk; Derby 'Lightweight', 2.50 pm Ipswich-Yarmouth (South Town), 13 July 1963.
The scene of my attempted photo-call on the first Wickham Saloon trip (see page 89), it is certainly the most remote of the stations on the line. *2911*

Below left Reedham Junction, Norfolk; Derby 'Lightweight', 4.00 pm Yarmouth (Vauxhall)-Norwich, 13 July 1963.
With a Norfolk church set typically amidst trees in lowland meadows drenched by sea air, the single line to Yarmouth boasts a halt that serves only a windmill and a pub - Berney Arms. The 20 mph speed limit on the Lowestoft route is for the sharp curve (note the check rail to guide the wheels) and the approach to the swing-bridge over the River Yare. The signal arm is hidden by a sighting board provided to assist sighting by the driver, a typical safety precaution. *2913*

Above right Acle, Norfolk; Class 31 No D5693, Leeds (Central)-Yarmouth (Vauxhall), 13 July 1963.
On the alternative route between Yarmouth and Brundall (and Norwich), Acle is a typical East Anglian wayside station complete with loop on the basic single track. The lights (electric!) are of LNER design. Some passengers are waiting for an up service that may cross here. *2912*

Below Whitwell & Reepham, Norfolk; Metro-Cammell 'Lightweight' No 79271, 1.32 pm Melton Constable-Norwich (City), 4 August 1958.
The train on the left is the first diesel multiple unit in which I ever travelled. Fame indeed! Harry, Alan and myself are on one of our circular tours, which aimed to cover most of BR: 9.30 am London (Liverpool Street)-Norwich Thorpe; 1.35 pm Norwich City-Melton

Constable; 2.30 pm from there to Wisbech North; 4.35 pm to Peterborough North; 5.40 pm to Stamford; 6.22 pm to Seaton; 6.56 pm to Peterborough North; and 8.02 pm to London (King's Cross). Harry's circular tour ticket cost much more than ours and had been wrongly routed via Seaton in Devon. A refund was forthcoming in due course!

Whitwell & Reepham was to be the first terminus used by us in the Wickham Saloon nearly 16 years later (see page 89). By then it was reached from Wroxham (only) by the Themelthorpe curve linking the former Great Eastern and Midland & Great Northern branches, and trains from Norwich approached from the north rather than the south, as at the time of the picture. The line carried traffic to and from the concrete works at Lenwade, the 'main' line having closed in 1959. *1376*

Dereham, Norfolk; Derby 'Lightweight', 2.20 pm Norwich-King's Lynn, 1 August 1960.
Dereham even has *tubular* electric lights - progress indeed, yet sadly it was to close in 1969. The Wickham Saloon came here too on our first charter (see page 88) and brought a family from Yaxham at their request. They opened (and closed) the crossing gates there for us, then climbed aboard. *2139*

Wendling, Norfolk; Derby 'Lightweight', 10.44 am Dereham-King's Lynn, 22 June 1963.
A modeller's dream station: station buildings, warehouse, signal box, platelayer's hut (concrete and new, so as to add to the losses that could be put on the branch ledger in anticipation of closure), loading gauge, telegraph poles and wires, signal wires, sidings, shunt signal, point lever and train. *2907*

Above Swaffham, Norfolk; Metro-Cammell 'Lightweight', 3.40 pm Thetford-Swaffham, 1 August 1960.

Swaffham, junction for Thetford, is an important expanding country town (now with a bypass). We are on our August Bank Holiday Monday Circular Tour from London Liverpool Street to King's Cross via Norwich, Wells-next-the-Sea, Dereham, Swaffham, Thetford, Ely north curve, March and Peterborough. Look at the yard and all the wagons; today this is the home of road haulage and a fine mess it was on my last visit. *2140*

Right Ashwell & Morden, Cambridgeshire; Class 105, 1.05 pm Cambridge-King's Cross, 19 November 1960.

A frequent service of electric trains now passes this way, and it is the principal route from London to Cambridge, the station serving up-market commuter land. If the line is electrified from Ely to Peterborough it could become an important diversionary route for the East Coast Main Line. Unfortunately this is rather a dull picture, and there is a telegraph pole growing out of the roof of the DMU. . . *2308*

Above Sandy, Bedfordshire; Class 31 No D5575, Walsall-Yarmouth (Vauxhall), 8 June 1963.

When there were great ideas for the development of the Oxford-Cambridge direct route during the BR modernisation plan of the 1950s, the bridge over the East Coast Main Line at Sandy was renewed, though for a single track only. Sadly it lost its trains at the beginning of 1968 and the bridge has already gone. Now electric trains pass beneath to and from King's Cross, and Sandy (ex-GNR) station has four tracks between its platforms. *2901*

Left Potton, Bedfordshire; Class 108, 2.00 pm Bletchley-Cambridge, 4 July 1964.

Potton was originally at the end of a short private railway from Sandy, which was later absorbed into the Oxford/Cambridge route. After closure the formation was used in part for a local authority drainage system. The availability of an uninterrupted route saves considerable sums of money for the local ratepayers. *3268*

Lord's Bridge, Cambridgeshire; Class 110, 4.47 pm Cambridge-Bletchley, 23 March 1963.
The scene here has been transformed by the Mullard Astronomy Unit as the railway happens to cross the Greenwich Meridian a little to the west.
There are now radio telescopes on either side of the station and more to the west, the buildings having become a small museum. The bridge from which
the picture was taken has been demolished and a fast major road now crosses the formation on the level. 2851

Above **King's Cliffe, Northamptonshire; Class 24 No D5079, 6.12 pm Peterborough East-Rugby, 27 August 1960.**
A slightly unbalanced picture, but the best I could do at the time. The station no longer exists and the line closed in 1968, but King's Cliffe remains a fascinating village with many old buildings and, to my mind, a medieval atmosphere in parts. There is a London & North Western Railway lower-quadrant signal for the train. Both buildings probably had awnings at one time that had become unsafe and were removed. *2220*

Below **Welham Junction, Northamptonshire; Class 24, 12.30 pm Rugby (Midland)-Peterborough East, 2 November 1963.**
Further west and amidst the fields is Welham Junction, with my favourite Joint line running north to Nottingham and Newark via Melton Mowbray through High Leicestershire, seen diverging to the right of the picture. The goods is waiting to enter the yard as the passenger passes eastbound. *3029*

Theddingworth, Leicestershire; Class 101, 12.26 pm Ely-Birmingham (New Street), 18 April 1964.
Still nearer Rugby is Theddingworth, with its LNWR lower-quadrant signal clear for the Birmingham train. Note too the complicated pointwork to gain access to the yard and bay platform. 3133

Above Cotham, Nottinghamshire; Class 105, RCTS 'Vale of Belvoir' Railtour, 29 April 1961.
There's an elaborate access to the sidings here, too. Because the station closed so long ago no attempt has been made to demolish the buildings - why bother, no one was going to vandalise them in those days - though the awnings have been removed for safety. My nephew is on the platform and has just photographed the lamp, complete with bird's nest, which has survived high on the corner of the building. *2394*

Left Heckington, Lincolnshire; Class 108, 10.33 am Skegness-Grantham, 20 April 1963.
Still very Great Northern at the time of this picture, two somersault signals guard the gated crossing. Heckington windmill dominates the scene. *2859*

Opposite page Barnetby, Lincolnshire; Class 114, Doncaster-Cleethorpes; Class 114, 2.33 pm New Holland (Pier)-Lincoln (Central), both 3 August 1959.
Not only is this one of the last junctions complete with semaphore signals in mainland Britain, but modellers will note the cattle pens on the right, the maltings on the left and the trackwork for the four roads that used to extend to Brocklesby. There is also a small shunt signal on the extreme right and a water column on the platform. *AL131/1759*

Above Mumby Road, Lincolnshire; Class 114, 1.40 pm Willoughby-Mablethorpe, 10 July 1965.
Yet more GNR somersault signals, guarding a bi-directional loop at a very wayside station where the landowner insisted that a Bible should always be available for passengers to consult. Although unstaffed and with a locked waiting room, a Bible was still visible on a table inside. The station closed in 1970. *3478*

Below Driffield, East Yorkshire; Class 110, Hull-Bridlington, 3 August 1964.
Last but not least in this section is Driffield, between Hull and Bridlington and served by trains to Scarborough. The junction signal guards both the route to Hull and to Selby via Market Weighton (closed in 1965). There is a substantial water tank to supply locomotives thirsty after their climb over the Wolds (perhaps from Malton too until 1958). Is the lamp in the foreground gas? The station sign is in bright North Eastern Region tangerine. *3284*

5.
THE DALES

Almost all the following pictures were taken in Yorkshire, Kipling Cotes being newly restored to the fold. There the house has become a teashop on a formation that is now a cycleway - and very nice too in the circumstances.

The Esk Valley Line is represented by Nunthorpe (page 56) and Sleights, where I witnessed the last coal delivery by train in 1983 during the first week of my retirement. Trains used to continue to Scarborough until 1965, when Ravenscar closed. There were high hopes when the line opened that a prosperous resort would develop here, but the inclement weather put a stop to that and the buildings

to the right of the station with their esplanade, and the surviving hotel, were all that came about. The view of Prospect Hill, Whitby (page 57), where trains from

Kipling Cotes, East Yorkshire; Class 105, Hull (Paragon)-York, 1 May 1964.

Etton Dale: I'm told that this remote station is now a teashop adjacent to a cycleway. Doesn't it look neat and tidy with provision for oil lamps to pick out the platform and to show the driver where to stop? It closed in 1965, having been unstaffed for about four years. Enthorpe station on the Driffield line was nearer Kipling Cotes racecourse, which, like Cartmel, normally has only an annual meeting. *3141*

Scarborough reversed in West Cliffe station, and joined those from Loftus going down to the seaside, includes some graceful North Eastern Railway lower-quadrant signals.

I have always considered the picture at Hebden Bridge as capturing the spirit of Calderdale and its dying industry; the loops have since been lifted, but there remain plenty of trains to Manchester, Blackpool and Leeds. Skelmanthorpe (page 60) reminds us of the Clayton West branch.

Much of the commuter traffic by road that congests the north side of Leeds could have been avoided had not the line from Arthington through Otley to Ilkley been closed in 1965. This was a very short-sighted decision in my view, though the formation has become useful as the Otley Bypass. Armistead (page 61) lies between Giggleswick and Clapham on the Settle Junction-Carnforth 'Little North Western' route.

Above Nunthorpe, Cleveland; Class 101, 9.26 am from Middlesbrough, 24 May 1960.
Teesside: Note the sharp drop of the tracks behind the train as they slope down to Middlesbrough. When we chartered the Civil Engineer's Saloon to Whitby an additional DMU had to be coupled to it to ensure it cleared the summit without problems; I was actually asked whether I would like it coupled to the front or the back, which I thought very considerate. *AL1078*

Above right Sleights, North Yorkshire; Class 101, Middlesbrough-Scarborough, 2 May 1964.
Eskdale: Note the ancient coach in the yard and the coal stocks; and I wonder whose trunk has been left by the guard. Wagons were still moved by manpower here in 1983.
This is the day of a special steam train over the line and I have come by car so as to follow it. At this time I frequently had dinner, bed and breakfast at the station house at Egton, sleeping in a room

above the former booking office; I had seen a B&B sign when using the train, and how lucky I was to take it up! On the first visit Mr Smith, then a guard, invited me to join the last train of the day from Whitby, which turned back as empty stock at Glaisdale. I rode back along in the darkened coaches and was duly set down at Egton by the kindly driver - a simple event that in memory I now greatly cherish. Later he was to become signalman at Grosmont Junction. His son-in-law, then a policeman, had started to write fiction and was later to be the author of the TV success *Heartbeat*, among many others. *3145*

Right Prospect Hill, Whitby, North Yorkshire; Class 101, Scarborough-Middlesbrough, 24 May 1960.
Eskdale: The line from Scarborough runs through the right-hand arch and this train had previously passed that way, reversing in Whitby's West Cliffe station in the distance. Do observe the graceful North Eastern Railway signals. *AL1077*

Ravenscar, North Yorkshire; Class 114, Scarborough-Whitby, 2 May 1964.
Staintondale: It's obvious that the North Eastern was by no means certain that Ravenscar was destined to be a resort, for all the buildings, and even the platform on the left, are of wood. The lantern contains no lamp and generally there is an air of decay. Closure was effected in 1965. *3147*

Scorton, North Yorkshire; Class 101, Richmond-Darlington, 12 April 1965.
Swaledale: Here the wooden platform is but an extension for longer trains. There is little else to say except that Scorton station is nearer Moulton than Moulton station; presumably they were named after the parishes in which they were situated. *3396*

Hebden Bridge, West Yorkshire; Class 110, Leeds-Manchester (Victoria), 8 May 1965.
Calderdale: Although the main road parallels the railway through the dale, there is plenty of traffic on each. I always enjoy a train ride this way, especially when en route to or from Blackpool with its Wurlitzer organ in the Tower Ballroom. 3436

Left Skelmanthorpe, West Yorkshire; Class 101, Clayton West-Huddersfield, 11 July 1964.

Denby Dale: One of the rare occasions when my professional life over-lapped with my enthusiast life involved this picture. The Rural District Council's Association published a resumé of one of the first rural transport conferences, held at the Central Hall, Westminster, in 1971, and used this as the cover picture. The conference Chairman was then one Tom King MP, later to become an important figure in Government circles. *3276*

Below left Pool-in-Wharfedale, West Yorkshire; Class 108, Leeds (Central)-Ilkley, 4 May 1963.

Wharfedale: Perched on the hillside with extensive views northwards, it is difficult to understand why this service was withdrawn. The local service had but two more years to operate, but could have met an up-market commuter need as well as providing an alternative route from Leeds to Ilkley. I made two journeys over it. On the first occasion Alan and I joined the 5.35 pm ex-Leeds at Arthington, having come from Harrogate, and later continued from Ilkley to Skipton for the night. The other time we were taking lunch aboard a steam special from York via the Derwent Valley, Tadcaster and Wetherby, which took the Arthington North Curve (while we were having soup) after reversal at Harrogate, and continued to Newcastle via the Settle & Carlisle and the Alston branch, on which we had dinner! *2865*

Above Armistead, North Yorkshire; Class 25 No D5224, 10.55 am Morecambe-Leeds, 24 April 1965.

Ribblesdale: The headcode '2N71' means that the train is heading for the North Eastern Region; it is currently in the London Midland Region. Because of the weather the superb view of Ingleborough from this point is obscured. I used to know the people who lived in the house and frequently drove there at one time. *3432*

Right The DMU tour to Ingleton shown in this advertising leaflet, a rare visit by such a unit to a station closed in 1954, would have passed Armistead.

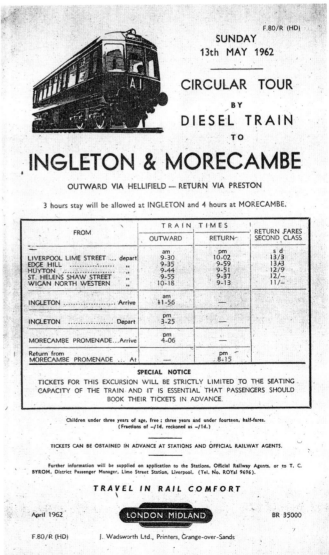

F.80/R (HD)

SUNDAY
13th MAY 1962

CIRCULAR TOUR

BY

DIESEL TRAIN

TO

INGLETON & MORECAMBE

OUTWARD VIA HELLIFIELD — RETURN VIA PRESTON

3 hours stay will be allowed at INGLETON and 4 hours at MORECAMBE.

FROM	TRAIN TIMES		RETURN FARES SECOND CLASS
	OUTWARD	RETURN	
	am	pm	s d
LIVERPOOL LIME STREET ... depart	9-30	10-02	13/3
EDGE HILL .... "	9-35	9-59	13/3
HUYTON "	9-44	9-51	12/9
ST. HELENS SHAW STREET "	9-55	9-37	12/-
WIGAN NORTH WESTERN "	10-18	9-13	11/-
INGLETON .... Arrive	am 11-56		
INGLETON .... Depart	pm 3-25	—	
MORECAMBE PROMENADE...Arrive	pm 4-06	—	
Return from MORECAMBE PROMENADE ... At	—	pm 8-15	

SPECIAL NOTICE

TICKETS FOR THIS EXCURSION WILL BE STRICTLY LIMITED TO THE SEATING CAPACITY OF THE TRAIN AND IT IS ESSENTIAL THAT PASSENGERS SHOULD BOOK THEIR TICKETS IN ADVANCE.

Children under three years of age, free ; three years and under fourteen, half-fares.
(Fractions of –/1d. reckoned as –/1d.)

TICKETS CAN BE OBTAINED IN ADVANCE AT STATIONS AND OFFICIAL RAILWAY AGENTS.

Further information will be supplied on application to the Stations, Official Railway Agents, or to T. C. BYROM, District Passenger Manager, Lime Street Station, Liverpool. (Tel. No. ROYal 9696).

TRAVEL IN RAIL COMFORT

April 1962   LONDON MIDLAND   BR 35000

F.80/R (HD)   J. Wadsworth Ltd., Printers, Grange-over-Sands

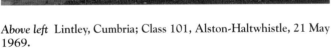

Special Excursion
BY
DIESEL TRAIN

CLEETHORPES

SUNDAY 5th AUGUST 1962

FROM	DEPARTURE TIMES	RETURN FARES SECOND CLASS	RETURN ARRIVAL TIMES
	am	s d	pm
MANCHESTER Piccadilly ...	9 50	21/-	10 16
GORTON & OPENSHAW ...	9 58	21/-	10 8
GUIDE BRIDGE ...	10 4	20/3	10 2
NEWTON for HYDE ...	10 9	19/9	9 56
BROADBOTTOM ...	10 14	19/6	9 50
DINTING ...	10 19	19/3	9 39
GLOSSOP ...	10x10	19/-	9x44
HADFIELD ...	10 24	19/-	9 35

CLEETHORPES ... ... arrive 1 13 pm

Return from CLEETHORPES ... ... at 7 0 pm

x—Change at HADFIELD outwards, DINTING on return.

SPECIAL NOTICE
Tickets for this Excursion will be Strictly Limited to the seating capacity of the train and Passengers are requested to Book their Tickets in Advance.

Children under three years of age free; three years and under fourteen, half-fare. (Fractions of a Penny reckoned as a Penny).

TICKETS CAN BE OBTAINED IN ADVANCE AT STATIONS AND OFFICIAL RAILWAY AGENTS

Further information will be supplied on application to Stations, Official Railway Agents, or to Mr. G. W. BRIMYARD, District Passenger Manager L.M.R., Hunts Bank, Manchester, 3. Telephone: BLA 3456. Ext. 587.

July, 1962.
Ernest Lee (Hyde) Ltd.   LONDON MIDLAND   XB/HD   BR 35000   E 586/HD

Above left Lintley, Cumbria; Class 101, Alston-Haltwhistle, 21 May 1969.
Tynedale: This is a glorious spot, at which I am looking forward to recording the narrow gauge steam train of the South Tynedale Railway when it reaches Slaggyford. The photograph is taken from the main road at a point where a sharp bend is involved and an abrupt climb south. *3660*

Left Birkett Tunnel, near north portal, Cumbria; Derby 'Lightweight', 8.35 am Carlisle-Skipton, 18 May 1966.
Eden Dale: This is typical limestone hill country through which the DMU is climbing out of Kirkby Stephen. We're waiting for the steam-hauled Long Meg-Widnes anhydrite gypsum freight, which normally followed this train, so the picture is really a make-weight! Notice how the phone wires are rising to pass above Birkett Tunnel. *3573*

Above left Woodhead Tunnel, Derbyshire; Class 114, diverted Sheffield-Manchester, 31 August 1969.
Longdendale: My fascination for railways was created in part by a ride behind steam through the Woodhead Tunnel on the former Great Central route over the Pennines - the narrow bore on the left of the double-track one that was brought into use in 1954 and declared redundant only 16 years later! It was on 2 May 1952 that from a station stop we puffed into that tunnel and into a wonderful world or railways that has led ultimately to this book. *C4462*

Above The DMU shown in this leaflet for an excursion to Cleethorpes would have gone through Woodhead Tunnel. Unusual routes and destinations are becoming uncommon today.

6.
SCOTLAND

There are so many pictures here that I cannot do justice to them all in this introductory text. I hope that you will feel that they truly reflect the various facets of that countryside. I'll mention just a few.

After one view of the Nithsdale route we concentrate on the Glasgow-Stranraer line, which, since closure of the direct route from Dumfries in 1965, has accommodated traffic from the south too, via Kilmarnock and Ayr.

Then to the Glasgow commuter area. Inverkip survives on the Wemyss Bay branch and has been electrified. Kilmacolm on the other hand, on the former Glasgow & South Western Railway route to Greenock, was retained as a terminus for a while, but eventually succumbed. Lesmahagow went too, in 1965.

The line from Lanark to Muirkirk has always seemed to me to be a forgotten railway; I have included three pictures. Built by the Caledonian, it met the GSWR end-on at Muirkirk and once carried a Saturday train from Dalmellington to Edinburgh via Carstairs. Closure throughout came in 1964, though passenger trains had been withdrawn at the western end in 1951.

Rumbling Bridge and Crook of Devon were on the Dollar Valley line and, prior to closure in 1964, saw only one train each way per day. Alan and I travelled over the route on the 4.15 pm from Glasgow (Queen Street High Level) on 29 May 1959. It was the only through train of the day and passed its opposite number at Alloa. We crossed the Forth by the swing-bridge at Throsk and our tickets were taken, in the time-honoured custom, at Bridge of Earn; Perth was an open station even then. There was no one else on the train. We had come from Kirkcudbright that day via Stranraer!

I recall the Waverley Route - Carlisle-Edinburgh - also in three pictures. Steele Road must be one of the loneliest stations. At Whitrope the train has stopped to set

down the signalman's wife who lives in the nearby cottages and has returned from shopping in Hawick. So have the residents of the station house at Stobs, but they used the Saturdays-only service to Riccarton Junction. They thought my tripod was a theodolite and that we had come to check the level of the footbridge.

Alan's picture on page 75 shows a Perth-Edinburgh train running via the most direct route through Glen Farg. Our Motorail train went that way on Saturday evening 22 July 1961 behind an 'A4' 'Pacific', puffing steadily up the hill with its 16-coach load of sleepers and car-carriers to King's Cross. There is a whiff of scandal behind the closure of this route in 1964. It had been shown as for retention and development on the 1967 map agreed by BR and the Ministry of Transport for the UK, but when an application for grant-aid was made by BR in 1968 the Minister contended that re-routing of the trains via Stirling would offer 'better value for money', and consent to closure was given in October 1969. A major consideration in the decision was the prospect of using the trackbed at Glen Farg to save the Scottish Roads Division £250-500,000 in constructing the M90 motorway. As Gourvish says (*British Railways 1948-73*, page 454), 'It is difficult to escape the conclusion that the Ministry acted both as judge and jury in the case.' Since closure, every passenger by rail has had some 20 miles added to his journey (and fare?).

The pictures of Glenbarry, Drummuir and Orton recall the alternative routes from Aberdeen to Inverness, via the coast, via Dufftown and via Mulben respectively, the latter being the only one left.

It seems right to end with pictures on the mountainous routes to Inverness, Oban and the Kyle of Lochalsh respectively.

Enterkinfoot, Dumfries & Galloway; Class 45, 4.10 pm Glasgow (St Enoch)–Leeds, 25 May 1964.

The headcode '1N63' means that this train is bound for the North Eastern Region. It was a service that always impressed me: out and back in a day. It left Leeds at 10.25 am, spent an hour in St Enoch station, then returned south. Simplicity itself - even a van included! Today the route through the Nith Valley sees only 'Sprinter' units unless there are diversions from the West Coast Main Line north of Carlisle. Once or twice each week the English China Clays/Caledonian Paper Mills tanker train passes this way between Burngullow near St Austell in Cornwall and the Ayrshire coast at Barassie. 3195

Above **New Luce, Dumfries & Galloway; Class 120, 4.40 pm Stranraer Town-Glasgow (St Enoch), 27 May 1964.**
Why BR took the trouble to close this station I shall never know. Only a few hundred yards from the village street, it should have had a regular, if small, clientele to and from Stranraer for shopping trips, if not for employment. I suspect that like Glenwhilly, the next station north, the powers that be had never visited the site to see the situation. *3209*

Below **Near Chirmorie, Strathclyde; Class 126, 9.00 am Glasgow (St Enoch)-Stranraer Town, 26 May 1964.**
One tends to think of the Scottish Highlands as the wildest places that railways penetrate in the UK. But the line south of Barrhill over isolated Chirmorie Summit and through Glenwhilly takes some beating! I took the car one day to a very lonely spot with a view to seeing the down and up boat trains around lunchtime, which used to cross at Glenwhilly station. A magnificent, cool, sunny day, there was total silence amidst the superb scenery with its extensive views to the north-east. The down train passed on time; then nothing more happened. Eventually a shepherd appeared with his flock. 'Are you waiting for the boat train?' he said. 'If so, it won't be here for a couple of hours as one of the boats from Larne has developed a fault this week.' I packed up my bag and saw the train near Pinwherry instead. *3198*

Pinmore Tunnel, near north portal, Strathclyde; Class 126, 11.25 am Glasgow (St Enoch)-Stranraer Harbour, 26 May 1964.
The train, having left the coast at Girvan, is climbing south through the hills towards the tunnel north of the former Pinmore station and a viaduct to its south.
As at Birkett Tunnel (page 62), the phone wires are routed above the tunnel. *3197*

Dailly, Strathclyde; Class 120, 2.30 pm Glasgow (St Enoch)-Girvan, 27 August 1965.
My car, GPJ 3C, is parked to the right in company with an old Daimler, which I assume belonged to the booking clerk. Large numbers of red roses are in bloom here, but the station closed in the autumn of this year and the permanent way has since been reduced to a single track. Needless to say, the signals have gone. *3504*

Inverkip, Strathclyde; Class 107, 6.20 pm Wemyss Bay-Glasgow (Central), 27 August 1965.
This location to the south-west of Glasgow is now part of the suburban electrified system and serves commuters into the city.
The wide space between the tracks suggests that a line was provided for non-stop trains at one time. Today just a single track suffices.
The vast station buildings have been replaced. *3507*

Kilmacolm, Strathclyde; Class 100, 10.55 am from Glasgow (St Enoch), 23 May 1964.
These more extensive station buildings were for Glasgow commuters west of the city who fought BR to retain their trains but lost in 1983. Look at the substantial houses on the left. *3189*

Lesmahagow, Strathclyde; Class 101, empty stock Coalburn-Stonehouse, 20 May 1964.
Another bleak and lonely area exists southeast of Glasgow, and it also contains coal seams, hence the number of lines seeking to carry away the mineral that gradually closed down as exploitation came to an end. Coalburn was to keep its limited train service for another 18 months when we made our visit. The morning trains went out empty stock and the evening ones returned in similar fashion. Our guard has suggested that the empty train stop here for photos and we have taken up the opportunity. Someone keeps the place clean! *3173*

Above left Sandilands, Strathclyde; Class 105, 10.55 am Lanark-Douglas West, 21 May 1964.

Left Happendon, Strathclyde; Class 105, 11.55 am Lanark-Muirkirk, 21 May 1964.

Above Inches, Strathclyde; Class 101, 8.48 pm Lanark-Muirkirk, 22 May 1964.

I would describe this as 'the forgotten railway', which lingered on until 1964 for passengers and 1966 for freight. As mentioned on the previous page, the line traverses lonely, bleak country, and for some miles it was obliged by the terrain to keep close company with the main Ayr-Edinburgh road (A70), which handles primarily through traffic. It is seen in the first two views in the upper Clyde Valley; a viaduct carrying the line over the river is just visible in the top centre of the view of Sandilands. Note the layout at Happendon (renamed by the LMS from Douglas) with its crane and mature trees. The third view at Inches (no village of that name is shown on the OS map) is seen late in the day as the sun was setting; 2 XPA is parked alongside the train.

I was ill the night we stayed at nearby Douglas; I had eaten corned beef in the refreshment room at St Enoch station. Next day food poisoning from such meat was announced at Aberdeen and I presume that I had had some from the same batch of tins. *3175/3176/3184*

Above Rumbling Bridge, Tayside; Class 101, 3.20 pm Alloa-Perth.
Left Crook of Devon, Tayside; same train, both 30 May 1964.
Because of the paucity of trains I have set down Alan from the car at Crook of Devon and returned to Rumbling Bridge - hence the same train in both photos! Do notice the tall North British lower-quadrant signal in the distance and the one nearer the camera at Rumbling Bridge. Only one train ran each way at this time, presumably for school children. *3226/AL1071*

Above Steele Road, Borders; Class 45 No D16, 9.15 am St Pancras-Edinburgh (Waverley) 'The Waverley', 28 May 1964.
Below Whitrope Summit, Borders; Class 27 No D5385, 2.43 pm Edinburgh (Waverley)-Carlisle, 20 July 1963.

This is Liberal Party country and I have always assumed that the Waverley route was closed (1969) partly to show the then Government's electoral superiority in numbers. What other reason could there be for shutting such an important trunk route linking the border towns with London? The duplication argument goes out of the window when you explore the route on the ground.

Steele Road station recalls memories of Peter Handford's masterly recordings of *Trains in the Night*, which won him an accolade in France and led to commissions in Italy among other places.

At Whitrope Summit at the head of Liddesdale the train has stopped to set down the signalman's wife on her return from shopping in Hawick. Note the Gresley brake and the van. *3214/2937*

Below Stobs, Borders; Class 26, 4.10 pm Edinburgh (Waverley)-Riccarton Junction, 20 July 1963.

The train drawing into Stobs did not appear in the public timetable, but was an extension of an Edinburgh/Hawick train on Saturdays to Riccarton Junction for the benefit of families resident there. I immediately hastened, via a pig sty, to the field track visible at the back of the photo so as to be ready to photograph the Carlisle/Millerhill freight due the other way 10 minutes later - followed by the empty stock of the passenger returning to Hawick.

My visit to Riccarton Junction is memorable. Until the Forestry Commission began to take over there was no road access. A rough track had been put in by 1968, so I decided to try my luck with the car. I advised the signalman at Kershopefoot of my intentions and he phoned his colleague at Riccarton. It was agreed that if I hadn't arrived there within an hour then I had had a puncture! In the event the going was good, a cup of tea was awaiting me in the signal box and I photographed the up 'Waverley'. The only inhabitant then was a lady who trained Doberman Pinscher dogs.

In an earlier attempt to get pictures at Riccarton I had joined an enthusiasts' special from Glasgow scheduled to make a photo-stop there. Imagine my anger when it steamed straight through in brilliant sunshine and called instead at Kershopefoot. I remonstrated there with the organiser who clearly had no idea of the stupidity of his action; his geographical knowledge was nil! *2940*

Below Reston, Borders; Class 40 No D249, 9.10 am Leeds (City)-Glasgow (Queen Street), 24 July 1963.

Today there is plain track at this location, but at least there are still trains - on the East Coast Main Line - and electric ones too. Reston was a great cattle mart and junction for the branch (to the right) from Duns (closed entirely in 1966). It used to be steam-worked from Tweedmouth except on Bank Holiday Mondays in England when a diesel came from Edinburgh. The train in the picture would have gone direct from Edinburgh to Glasgow, not by way of Carstairs as now. *2962*

Glenfarg, Tayside; Class 26 (x2), 10.50 am Perth-Edinburgh, 17 May 1964.
Two locomotives were necessary for the stiff climb up Glen Farg - now the car sails up in top gear on the substitute motorway, though with much less weight to carry. See page 64 for more detail. *AL1073*

Laurencekirk, Grampian; Class 24 No D5130, 5.30 pm Aberdeen-Perth, 27 May 1966.
Why has there been no local service south from Aberdeen since the stopping trains to Perth via Forfar were withdrawn in 1967? It's incredible to me that all trains calling at Stonehaven link it with London, Edinburgh or Glasgow - if Stonehaven remains open, why not Laurencekirk (closed in 1967) where the station was sited right in the town?

I love the dappled effect of the evening sun on the station. There used to be a wagon turntable here because of the restricted space in the yard. Note the semaphore signals in the distance sited high in the air so that the footbridge did not impede the driver's view. *3596*

Above left Glenbarry, Grampian; Class 21 No D6139, 9.30 am Elgin-Aberdeen via the coast, 10 July 1961.
Left Drummuir, Grampian; Class 26, 3.55 pm Elgin-Aberdeen via Dufftown, 10 July 1961.
Above Orton, Grampian; Class 120, 8.30 am Inverness-Aberdeen via Mulben, 10 July 1961.

These three trains are making their separate ways to Aberdeen from Elgin via Cairnie Junction. The type of locomotive at Glenbarry (closed in 1968) did not have a high reputation and was soon phased out. At Drummuir I believe that the track is still in situ between Keith and Dufftown. *2476/2484/AL1331*

Above Kincraig, Grampian; Class 25 D5125 + unidentified Class 25, 8.20 pm up 'Royal Highlander', 11 July 1961.
The old gentleman (seen through the lantern) has taken up his nightly seat with his dog to observe the 'gentry ' making their way south to London, while a goods train is waiting in the loop for the road ahead. Kincraig station closed in 1965 but the loop survives. Alan and I had bed and breakfast here and wandered down to the station after dinner. Today the village has the advantage of not being on the A9 and can only be reached by a positive digression at Kingussie or Aviemore. *AL1454*

Above right Tyndrum Lower, Central; Class 21 Nos D6129 + D6100, 12 noon Glasgow (Buchanan Street)-Oban, 14 July 1961.
If you look closely you will see the West Highland line to Fort William above the train, marked by scattered bushes and one of Forman's viaducts. The two routes are parallel between Crianlarich and Tyndrum. *2457*

Right Near Achnasheen, Highland; Class 26 No D5335, 9.15 am Inverness-Kyle of Lochalsh, 21 July 1961.
Two pictures on the Kyle of Lochalsh route end the chapter. The first shows a train approaching Achnasheen with the 'Devon Belle' observation car at the rear. At that time the turntable survived at the Kyle for turning it. *AL1066*

Glencarron Platform, Highland; Class 25, Inverness-Kyle of Lochalsh freight, 21 July 1961.
Glencarron Platform was perhaps unique in that the building there contained levers by which you could put the signals at danger if you wished to join a train.
This has all disappeared, though the trains still pass through. *AL1069*

7.
SPECIAL TRAINS

The special focus at Bricket Wood (below) is really on the steam train, but it provides my only picture of the British United Traction units.

The Inter-City unit at Quainton Road (page 82) is one of my charters for the 'Talking of Trains' evening class at Surbiton, then in its ninth year. We are on our way from Clapham Junction to Derby, calling also at Harrow-on-the-Hill (where the LT ticket collector tried to debar one of our passengers from passing the barrier) and Clipston & Oxenden between Northampton and Market

Bricket Wood, Hertfordshire; British United Traction four-wheel units, 2.25 pm Watford Junction-St Albans (Abbey), 27 April 1958.

It has to be said that originally the diesel train was not the prime object of the photo, but in retrospect it is the more important feature. Time has made the Gresley coaches of the RCTS Special of similar interest; their locomotive is '2P' 0-4-4T No 41901 and the itinerary from London Fenchurch Street to Broad Street was via Stepney, South Tottenham and Stanmore, returning via St Albans (Abbey), Hertford North and East, Angel Road and Victoria Park. The branch is now electrified. *1221*

Harborough. We passed over the famous viaduct at Bletchley and went by way of Coalville, though this was by no means certain until we reached the outskirts of Leicester.

As far as I know, the Ian Allan Special (page 83) was the only DMU ever to traverse the M&GN main line. Harry, Alan and I happened to get the front seats on leaving King's Cross and enjoyed a superb view of the route from Peterborough onwards. We called at Wisbech, Sutton Bridge, South Lynn, Fakenham and Honing to cross service trains. We returned from Yarmouth (Beach) to North Walsham and transferred there to the route through Wroxham for Norwich and London.

Three pictures of the same Railway Enthusiasts' Club special (pages 84-5) may seem unbalanced, but that Club contributed so much to my enjoyment of railways that I see no reason to apologise. Keadby Wharf is an unusual place to visit. So was Barton-on-Humber at the time, but

this has now become the transfer point for buses to Hull by the Humber Bridge. In so doing it has superseded New Holland Pier, from where paddle-steamers used to ply regularly to Hull; a funnel can be seen in the picture.

Apart from a school special, the DMU at Hovingham (page 86), a rare occurrence in its own right, was the last to call. Normal service had been withdrawn in 1931, though holiday trains came this way from Scotland to the East Coast reversing twice, in a sense, at Malton.

It was unusual for BR to let a passenger train use track in the condition it was at Queensbury (page 87); someone must have pulled strings. There was a rusty hole in the footbridge and a cow on the platform at which passengers are alighting. Queensbury had once been a triangular junction, and we are on the Bradford (Exchange)-Keighley curve. The branch went to Halifax through a tunnel so deep below the surface that at one time it was used for measuring earthquakes.

Quainton Road, Buckinghamshire; Class 123, Clapham Junction-Derby Special, 27 September 1969.
At the time I thought it a novel idea to charter an Inter-City DMU for our tour into London Midland territory, but I was to regret it for apparently only Western Region drivers knew how to handle the units. I had also not been advised that the new Trent signal box was to be commissioned that day, with consequent disruption to normal services and the use of the goods lines south of Trent Junction with inevitable delays due to speed restrictions. Hence the driver from Reading booked to take us home was caught up in the muddle and we left late from Derby. Booked via Oakham, we had to go that way

because I was staying the night there. The look on the faces of Alan and Harry - who officially shared responsibility with me for running our specials - when they realised that they had to take over the running of the late train was an education to me as to the amount of hard work I had previously undertaken as a matter of course!

I'm disturbed that a passenger has obviously alighted on the 'wrong' side at Quainton Road; normally we were a very disciplined crowd. The poster in the left-hand window is advocating the retention of small district councils to avoid administration becoming too remote; a report on the reform of local government had just been published and the lobbying had begun. 3676

Wisbech North, Cambridgeshire; Class 105, King's Cross-Yarmouth (Beach) Ian Allan Special, 4 October 1958.
Quite a crowd is enjoying the spectacle of a DMU on the Midland & Great Northern route. Today Wisbech still has a railhead for goods by way of the former Great Eastern outlet to March. AL926

Above Keadby, Lincolnshire; Class 114, 'North Lindseyman' REC Special.
Above right Barton-on-Humber, Lincolnshire; same train.
Right New Holland (Pier), Lincolnshire; same train, all 21 April 1963.

These three pictures of the same Railway Enthusiasts' Club Special are all by Alan because I am now engaged more in colour photography and have no tripod with me to take two pictures at once. However, I have included them because of the interesting locations. It must also have been the only occasion when Fountain Coaches of Popesgrove, Twickenham in Middlesex, have provided an inter-station link for connecting passengers between Thorne North and Thorne South. At New Holland Pier it is unusual for the DMU to stand at the platform used by cars to reach the ferry service. Between it and the van are small wagons to which coal has been trans-shipped for use on the 'paddlers'. *AL555/AL550/AL551*

Above Hovingham, North Yorkshire; Class 104, 9.40 am Bradford (Forster Square)-Kirkbymoorside, 3 May 1964.
Just look at the genuine old-time ramblers alighting at Hovingham! Because of the route and reversal at Gilling I was also able to take pictures at Kirkdale and Kirkbymoorside. Little did I dream then that one day I would live near there! *3152*

Left A handbill advertising the ramblers' excursion.

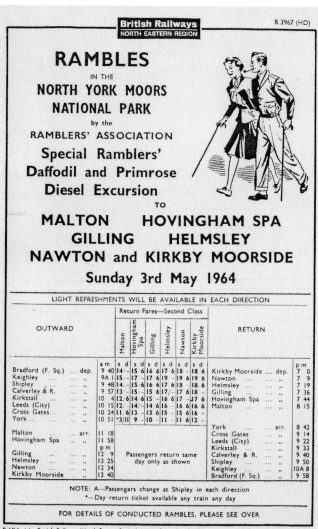

British Railways
NORTH EASTERN REGION

R 3967 (HD)

RAMBLES
IN THE
NORTH YORK MOORS
NATIONAL PARK
by the
RAMBLERS' ASSOCIATION

Special Ramblers'
Daffodil and Primrose
Diesel Excursion
TO

MALTON   HOVINGHAM SPA
GILLING   HELMSLEY
NAWTON and KIRKBY MOORSIDE
Sunday 3rd May 1964

LIGHT REFRESHMENTS WILL BE AVAILABLE IN EACH DIRECTION

OUTWARD		Malton	Hovingham Spa	Gilling	Helmsley	Nawton	Kirkby Moorside	RETURN	
	am	s d	s d	s d	s d	s d	s d		p m
Bradford (F. Sq.) ... dep.	9 40	14/-	15 6	16 6	17 6	18 -	18 6	Kirkby Moorside ... dep.	7 0
Keighley ... ... „	9A 1	15.-	17 -	17 6	19 -	19 6	19 6	Nawton ... ... „	7 9
Shipley ... ... „	9 48	14.-	15 6	16 6	17 6	18 -	18 6	Helmsley ... ... „	7 19
Calverley & R. ... „	9 57	13 -	15 -	15 6	17/-	17 6	18 -	Gilling ... ... „	7 36
Kirkstall ... ... „	10 4	12.6	14 6	15 -	16 6	17 -	17 6	Hovingham Spa ... „	7 44
Leeds (City) ... ... „	10 15	12.-	14/-	14 6	16 -	16 6	16 6	Malton ... ... „	8 15
Cross Gates... ... „	10 24	11.6	13 -	13 6	15 -	15 6	16 -		
York ... ... „	10 51	*3/11	9 -	10 -	11 -	11 6	12 -		
								York ... ... arr.	8 42
Malton ... ... arr.	11 18							Cross Gates ... „	9 14
Hovingham Spa ... „	11 58							Leeds (City) ... „	9 22
	p m							Kirkstall ... ... „	9 33
Gilling ... ... „	12 9		Passengers return same					Calverley & R. ... „	9 40
Helmsley ... ... „	12 25		day only as shown					Shipley ... ... „	9 50
Nawton ... ... „	12 34							Keighley ... ... „	10A 8
Kirkby Moorside ... „	12 40							Bradford (F. Sq.) ... „	9 58

NOTE: A—Passengers change at Shipley in each direction
*—Day return ticket available any train any day

FOR DETAILS OF CONDUCTED RAMBLES, PLEASE SEE OVER

Queensbury, West Yorkshire; Class 110, Bradford (Exchange)-Thornton RCTS Special, 6 September 1964.
An unbelievable scene at a once proud junction serving a village that was to produce a Vice-Chairman of British Rail. 3314

8.
PUTTING ON THE STYLE

Saxilby, Lincolnshire; Wickham Saloon, Selby-Womersley-Finningley-Lincoln; 3 May 1975.
Our patron, Bert Gemmell MBE, then Chief Passenger Manager, BR (Eastern), and later creator of 'The Sidings' restaurant north of York, has taken himself on to the buffer of the saloon; by chance my friend Harry is passing by on the platform. The destination blind, set for 'Mildenhall', had survived from operating days in East Anglia and we had innocent fun changing it from time to time in the most unlikely places! At Lincoln we transferred to the London express, to which had been added a dining car for breakfast on the outward run and dinner on the return. C6152A

Two events of particular significance to me occurred in the spring of 1974. On 1 April a major reorganisation of the administrative areas of local government took place in England and Wales and provided me with an enhanced salary and prospects. Then the preceding day, no doubt with the latter in mind, Bert Gemmell MBE, Chief Passenger Manager, BR Eastern Region, entertained me to lunch in York and, much to my surprise and delight, invited me to hire the saloon then used by the General Manager for inspections and the like. I was to learn subsequently at the Department that I owed this privilege to their enquiry into the cost of its operation, and by hiring it to me it was no longer exclusive to the GM's account!

The saloon is relevant to this book in being one of only a handful of early DMUs built by the Wickham Company of Ware in Hertfordshire. After operation in East Anglia it was transformed for the GM in 1967 to include a boardroom, bar, kitchen and seating area with settees and armchairs. The destination blinds remained in situ. The riding qualities also remained unchanged. I was warned by Gerry Fiennes, a previous incumbent at York, not to have formal meals on the move, and I later noted from a WTT (Working Timetable) that when some Japanese businessmen hired the saloon and had lunch en route to the Shildon celebrations, it was shunted on to the Wensleydale branch at Northallerton and remained stationary for an hour or so.

The fortunate passengers on my charters were mainly members of my 'Talking of Trains' evening class at Surbiton, then in its 14th year. For their convenience the saloon was brought to London for a trip on 20 July 1974.

In preparing the itinerary I was conscious that the Eastern Region was in one of the moods when passenger trains were not allowed to use lines restricted to freight traffic. The saloon, it seemed to me, was entitled to go anywhere, so it was agreed that it might run from Liverpool Street to Lowestoft, on to Norwich, then over

Near Burton Lammas, Norfolk; inside Wickham Saloon, Norwich-Whitwell & Reepham, 20 July 1974.
Teatime for Mr and Mrs Simon Davies (foreground), who had kindly provided my lunch, and Mrs Yvette Harvey,
on our first outing. C5783

the goods-only line from Wroxham to Whitwell & Reepham. Later it would go over another route restricted to freight, from Wymondham to Dereham and back and return home via Cambridge.

We were ready to leave Liverpool Street before time, but a train in the adjoining platform had an excess of coaches and blocked our exit. This caused consternation amongst those waiting at our platform to board the continental boat train and we had to repel boarders. Late departure and the failure of the signalman at Ipswich to realise that we were pathed to Norwich via Lowestoft and not direct, with consequent further delay, ruined my plan for a photographic stop at Brampton to coincide with the passing of an up holiday express.

Harry was concerned at the limited catering arrangements. Bert had authorised us to bring milk, coffee, tea and biscuits, and advised that if we approached the driver - after Shenfield, for some reason that I have never fathomed - he would give us the key to the kitchen. Those readers familiar with railway geography will know the down gradient towards Chelmsford and the pan of near-boiling milk resembled Vesuvius in eruption.

Lunch could be in picnic form, but what about dinner? I reconnoitred stations west of Wymondham to find one with an adjacent hotel. Brandon boasted 'The Great Eastern' and, equally important, a siding in which to stable the saloon. The hotel manager viewed my request for dinner for 33 *train* passengers with some scepticism but finally agreed, provided that I promised to phone if we were running late and on condition that we had a cold starter so that this could be set out in advance. In the event we arrived early and had more than 90 minutes to enjoy our meal.

The return from Cambridge to Liverpool Street took less than an hour, with due regard for speed restrictions, and concluded the first of many memorable days out in saloons, which could form the subject of a book in themselves.

Until 1980 we hired the Wickham Saloon twice almost every year. When originating in York, the King's Cross-Leeds sleeper was extended for us so that we could take advantage of it and make an early start. In September 1977 we travelled north only (from King's Cross to York via Bayford, Cambridge, Postland and

Cotham) and returned by service train. This was the sequel to a special run that week for the Planning Committee of the ADC (Association of District Councils) to visit the first garden city at Letchworth and to experience an electric train from Hertford North to Gordon Hill. The saloon remained stationary for lunch at a signal midway between Hitchin and our destination for the maximum period not to delay the normal hourly service.

Then by 1980 two more events had happened. Mr Gemmell had become Director, Public Affairs, in Scotland in anticipation of some devolution of power from Westminster, and the Wickham Saloon had been replaced by the Stourton Saloon, with much the same interior but of somewhat less quality. It too was a DMU and I was privileged to charter it regularly for the Friends of the National Railway Museum when I became their Secretary on my retirement from local government in 1983. On Tuesday 8 May 1984, for instance, we ran an evening trip from York to Redmire with dinner at Castle Bolton. Return was at 9.45 pm, in the twilight on a branch normally open only during daylight hours, and the GM, who was one of the guests, sadly saw scope for economies!

Meanwhile an invitation had come from Scotland to hire two individual saloons there and to couple them to a diesel locomotive for a day's outing. One of the shunters on our inaugural run from Perth advised me that coach No 1999 was destined ultimately for the National Railway Museum; it is now in private hands. In my expe-

rience it is unique in having a corridor connection at one end only, so that there is an unimpeded view to the rear. Even the coathooks breathe quality.

Our first tour was to Forfar and back, then to Carlisle via Newburgh, Cowdenbeath, Alloa and Dumfries with delay at Polmadie to change crew in an era of industrial disputes. There was some doubt as to whether signalmen would forego their football match and turn up to allow us to traverse the line from Townend Upper Junction at Dunfermline to Stirling, but in the event all went well. As we were running ahead of time at our photo-stop at Thornhill, I asked the driver whether he would add a stop at Annan. He was pleased to refuse. I had in mind to remind him then that he had greatly exceeded the speed limit through Kilmarnock, but thought better of it. Mrs Thatcher was about to come to the rescue or to create mayhem, depending on your point of view! The service train home had an engine failure at Wigan, but provided a good dinner.

The next tour encompassed Inverness, Burghead, Dufftown, Aberdeen and Dundee, but I failed to include

Redmire, North Yorkshire; Stourton Saloon, York-Redmire FNRM Special, 8 May 1984.
Amongst the passengers are a Viscount, a Regional Director of the Midland Bank, a former General Manager of BR (Eastern), a Deputy Director of the BR Property Board, the Chairman of the Friends' Company, and the editor of the Newsletter; the lady third from the left is Mrs Joyce Douglas (Auntie Joyce) who held the Friends' office together when I was Secretary. We are about to join the coach to take us to dinner in Castle Bolton. *Gavin Mist*

Brechin on the incorrect assumption that it would outlast the other branches. The loco ran short of water near Newtonmore and had to be shut down, followed by a cautious run to Aviemore to be replenished. After a lengthy signal check at Ardgaith, dinner was taken in the Station Hotel, Perth. Again we used sleepers from Euston to Perth and return.

On 25 April we reached perfection in our charters, having added a kitchen and a dining car to our two saloons, and enjoyed breakfast, lunch and dinner on board. This meant that we could have aperitif drinks on No 1999 and walk through to the diner for meals. As the other saloon had no corridor connection I had to arrange appropriate photo-stops so that guests could move in and out of the diner. On this first trip - from Glasgow (Queen Street) to Glenfinnan and Oban - we called at Garelochhead and Bridge of Orchy for breakfast, Rannoch after lunch, which began eastbound from Fort William, and Ardlui after dinner, which was served on leaving Oban.

Our last trip in Scotland was in 1985. Subsequently we were priced out of that market. The runs from York continued, however, but in due course the Stourton Saloon, too, was condemned and we travelled in the Civil Engineer's Saloon until this also came to its end. We were

destined to be on its last revenue-earning journey and our saloon outings ended in unusual style on 12 October 1991.

The itinerary was York-Normanton-Barnsley-Sheffield-Alfreton-Melton Mowbray-Kettering; return to Oakham; then ahead to Peterborough and home via Sleaford and Selby. Something parted from the unit near Dore and at Oakham the driver advised me that it was likely to be condemned at Peterborough as the speedometer was not working at one end. Instead a Class 47 was attached and our two coaches wasted no time between stops. A potential problem at Selby was avoided by a helpful driver and the Canal Curve. We watched the unit with its loco go north past 'The Sidings' that evening during dinner at the restaurant that had been started by the very same person who had authorised our first saloon trips.

Heckington, Lincolnshire; Stourton Saloon, York-Askern-Lowfield-Ancaster-Skegness, 20 September 1986.
We saw a service train at Heckington on page 52. Now the saloon has arrived on a much sunnier day; neither of the signals has retained its somersault arm, but the gated crossing is still there and the Great Northern signal box. Mr Kenneth Mellor, a member of my Harrow WEA class, is approaching the camera; I would like to renew contact but have mislaid his address. C5998

Above left Sleaford, Lincolnshire; BR(E) Civil Engineer's Saloon with Class 47, Peterborough-Lincoln-Doncaster-Selby-York, 12 October 1991.
Across the flower-beds stands *Horwich Enterprise*, which came to our rescue at Peterborough with a kindly driver who invited passengers to join him on the footplate; a rota was established to ensure parity of treatment between stops. C5994/4

Left Orbliston Junction, Grampian; two saloons and Class 26, Burghead-Aberdeen-Dundee-Perth, 26 April 1980.
It became our practice to take a group photo en route, and where better than by the gorse bushes in full flower at Orbliston (closed 1964), junction for Fochabers Town (closed to passengers 1931, to goods 1966)? The residents were happy to see us. This is the 'test' picture. C10781

Above Invershin Viaduct, Highland; two saloons, kitchen car and Class 26 No 26041, Inverness-Wick, 24 April 1982.
This picture may have been taken by David Pickett, a helpful stalwart of the 'Talking of Trains' class rather than by my camera. I had alerted the owner of the nearby Invershin Hotel, who I had met professionally, of our intention to run up and down the viaduct for photos in case his guests wished to join in. It is forbidden to walk across the viaduct and Bert Gemmell spent much time attempting to discourage trespassers. In vain, however, for I saw someone coming across on 16 August 1996; it is miles around by road and a proper footpath amidst the girders would seem a good idea. C11122

Corrour, Highland; two saloons, dining car, kitchen and Class 27 No 27034, Glasgow (Queen Street)-Glenfinnan, 25 April 1981.
I really like this picture, taken at a station so remote that only backpackers are likely to be found there. By virtue of radio control of the trains the signals have since been removed. We are about to cross the Mallaig-Glasgow (Queen Street) train and the air is fresh and gorgeous. There may be snow on the mountains but it's warm in our saloon as we look out over Rannoch Moor, and breakfast is sustaining us until coffee time! C11311

Barrhill, Dumfries & Galloway; two saloons, dining car, kitchen car and Class 27 No 27037, Largs-Ayr-Stranraer, 12 May 1984.
When intermediate stations to Stranraer were under threat of closure a fight was put up by the residents of Barrhill and their station was saved, even though it was high above the village and hardly convenient. I asked the Scottish Region whether the platforms were intact at Glenwhilly station with a view to stopping there for photographs. They said no, but a stop could be made at Dunragit on our return. Needless to say there proved to be no platforms there, but they had survived at Glenwhilly! Why hadn't I gone and looked? C9857

INDEX